THE STICK WIFE

by

DARRAH CLOUD

Dramatic Publishing
Illinois • London, England • Melbourne, Australia

to LQC

THE STICK WIFE was nominated for *Plays in Process* by Mame Hunt, Literary Manager of Los Angeles Theatre Center, where it was presented from January 2 through March 1, 1987.

Roberta Levitow directed. The set, costumes and lighting were designed by Pavel M. Dobrusky, and sound by Jon Gottlieb. The cast was as follows:

Ed Bliss	*Gene Ross*
Jessie Bliss	*Anne Gee Byrd*
Marguerite Pullet	*Chris Weatherhead*
Big Albert Connor	*Larry Drake*
Betty Connor	*Camilla Carr*
Tom Pullet	*Richard Dean*

Following the LATC production, *THE STICK WIFE* was produced by Hartford Stage Company in the spring of 1987. The version of the play circulated by *Plays in Process* was revised by the author as of June 1987.

THE STICK WIFE

A Full Length Play
For Three Men and Three Women

CHARACTERS

JESSIE BLISS . . . . housewife, 40-50
ED BLISS . . . . her husband, a mechanic
MARGUERITE PULLET . . . . housewife, younger than Jessie
TOM PULLET . . . . her husband, a truck driver
BETTY CONNOR . . . . housewife, 40-50
BIG ALBERT CONNOR . . . . her husband, a mechanic

TIME:
1963.

PLACE:
The backyard of the Bliss home in Birmingham, Alabama.

Playwright's Note

The "shadows of light" which appear at various points in the play are, literally, ghosts. I think of them as the "truth." Whether they are projections of Jessie's imagination or not, they exist on the material plane; they manifest themselves in some physical way. Formless holograms would be perfect, but that's for the future. In the Hartford Stage Company production, they were "ghost dogs." Whines were heard, gates rattled. At one point, a ghost dog trotted through the yard, indicated only by "footsteps" raising dust. The last manifestation was merely a great howling in the distance.

ACT ONE

SCENE ONE

SCENE: *A maze of clothesline stretches across the shoddy backyard. Drab work clothes hang from the line. The junk of marriage lies around. There are tubs or something else to sit on. A long wooden rifle-box serves as a step to the back door of the house. There is another exit leading to an alley.*

AT RISE: *September 1963. Early Sunday morning. ED enters in T-shirt and boxer shorts and takes clothes off the line. JESSIE enters in an old robe.*

JESSIE. Where ya goin'? *(Pause; ED dresses.)* Ed?...Where ya goin'? *(He pays no attention to her.)* Ed?...Ed?...Ed?... Where ya goin'?

ED. Don't ask me where I'm goin'. *(Pause.)*

JESSIE. When you comin' back? *(Pause; no answer.)* What about breakfast?

ED. What about it?

JESSIE. Thought I'd make apple pancake.

ED. Suit yourself.

JESSIE. I need to know when you'll be back so's I know when to start it. *(Pause.)* It'll be ready 'round...ten o'clock!

ED. I won't be here.

JESSIE. Eleven?

ED. Still won't be here.

7

JESSIE. What time then?

ED. Don't know.

JESSIE. Yes, you do.

ED. Do not!

JESSIE. I don't know when to start it, there won't be any breakfast.

ED. So?

JESSIE. I could start it when I think you'll be back and if you're not back by then I'll eat it and save the rest and heat it up for you when you get home but it won't be as good.

ED. Do what you want.

JESSIE. I want to have breakfast with you! *(Pause.)*

ED. Won't be here. *(JESSIE trembles with rage; ED watches her stiffly; she grabs the hem of her robe and rips it at him.)*

JESSIE *(displaying it)*. I tore my robe! I tore my robe!

ED. You don't get another.

JESSIE. Where you goin'?

ED. Out.

JESSIE. You go, I won't be here when you get back.

ED. Yeah, you will.

JESSIE. Maybe not.

ED. Yeah, you will.

JESSIE. Maybe not!

ED. You always gonna be right where you are.

JESSIE. MAYBE NOT! *(Pause.)*

ED. Where ya goin? *(Pause.)*

JESSIE. Nowhere.

ED. Where?

JESSIE. Nowhere.

ED. Right.

JESSIE. I'm gonna follow you!

ED. Don't do it!

JESSIE. I'm gonna!

ED. I said no!

JESSIE. Why not?

ED. 'Cause you can't protect yourself. And I'm not gonna be lookin' out for you. Somebody might just come up behind you and snatch your life away from you. Just grab it like a pocketbook and run.

JESSIE. No, they wouldn't.

ED. Not worth grabbin', huh?

JESSIE. I raised two children!

ED. Yeah? Where are they?

JESSIE. You don't know anymore'n I do!

ED. I didn't raise 'em for nothin'!

JESSIE. They'll come back.

ED. Not since you poisoned 'em against me.

JESSIE. Don't say that!

ED. It's a free country. *(He starts to go.)*

JESSIE. Don't go! Ed! Don't go!

ED. You knew where I was goin' you wouldn't say that.

JESSIE. Don't go! Please! Please, don't go!

ED. See there? You don't know nothing'. *(ED exits to the alley; JESSIE watches after him a moment, then turns to look at the house.)*

SCENE TWO

AT RISE: *That afternoon. The phone is ringing. JESSIE enters and hangs nothing but white sheets on the line, ignores the phone. Eventually it stops ringing.*

JESSIE. Gary Cooper? Yes, I knew him…I worked with him on a number of pictures…he had a very rare skin disease…

his skin was like Saran Wrap...we starlets were afraid ta kiss him for fear of suffocatin'...My mother was the one got me into show business...my children were taken from me because of it...All my life I wanted those plastic plates, and when I finally got 'em, I used 'em on the kids..."affected" their cells...they were never the same after that...I don't know what happened to 'em...they never call...I think they're lyin' dead somewhere in a rest area named for an explorer up north...I have dreams...dreams that don't come from sleep...

(A shadow of light appears at one side of the stage. JESSIE sees it out of the corner of her eye; she turns to look at it and it disappears. Suddenly, MARGUERITE rushes on from the alley.)

MARGUERITE. I could hear you over here not answerin' the phone! *(JESSIE drops the laundry and heads for the house.)* Where you goin'? Jessie! Where you goin'? *(JESSIE freezes.)* Don't go!...Don't go! Please don't go!...You hear the news? *(JESSIE dashes for the house.)* Where you goin'? Jessie?

JESSIE. Don't ask me where I'm goin'!

MARGUERITE. Don't leave me!

JESSIE. Thank you, Marguerite, good-bye.

MARGUERITE. Jessie, please!

JESSIE. I have to go inside now!

MARGUERITE. I'll go with you!

JESSIE. No!

MARGUERITE. Please!

JESSIE. I'll call ya.

MARGUERITE. Don't make me know it, don't make me know it all alone.

JESSIE. Don't you dare come close to me with news on you!

MARGUERITE. It hurts!

JESSIE. Serves you right for knowin' it!

MARGUERITE. Only reason I turned my TV on was to send out my beam. Touch somebody important! Tell 'em, welcome, welcome to my livin' room! I am with you! You're in *my* house! And they give me the news!

JESSIE. Go home! Get outa here! *(She starts pushing MARGUERITE.)*

MARGUERITE. I'm not ready yet! *(They begin slapping at each other.)*

JESSIE. Leave me alone! Leave me alone! Leave me alone! Leave me alone!

MARGUERITE. Stop it! Stop it! Ow! Stop it! I'm not goin'! Stop it! Ow! *(They back off, panting.)*

JESSIE. It's my house!

MARGUERITE. I'll tell Ed on you!

JESSIE. You don't never believe what I want!

MARGUERITE. You'll be all right if you don't get what you want! But me, I'll expire! I'll just expire! *(They quiet down, warily.)* Somebody bombed a colored church. *(JESSIE pulls her dress up over her head.)* I'm sorry! I'm sorry! I just couldn't hold it in!

JESSIE. I don't wanna be here.

MARGUERITE. I have to be, you do!... Take your dress down, Jessie, I can't see you!

JESSIE. I'm not here!

MARGUERITE. Then I'm goin' home! *(MARGUERITE stands still; JESSIE whips her dress down.)*

JESSIE. Was anybody hurt?

MARGUERITE. I turned it off before they said.

JESSIE. Thank the Lord.

MARGUERITE. I didn't hear a word! I promise!

JESSIE. I predict those people are gonna get back at us.

MARGUERITE. We gonna hafta protect ourselves.

JESSIE. I can't! I don't know how!

MARGUERITE. We didn't even know what happened 'til the television. We's innocent and they's gonna come after us.

JESSIE. Colored have TV?

MARGUERITE. Not many, I expect.

JESSIE. Then how do they know what we know?

MARGUERITE. Lock your doors, Jessie.

JESSIE. Ed locks them.

MARGUERITE. Don't go out alone at night.

JESSIE. Oh, I never do.

MARGUERITE. Well I never do, either.

JESSIE. Not like I don't want to.

MARGUERITE. You don't want to go out alone at night!

JESSIE. Sometimes I do.

MARGUERITE. You don't really!

JESSIE. Sometimes.

MARGUERITE. Not really.

JESSIE. I do.

MARGUERITE. *I* couldn't.

JESSIE. Yes, you could.

MARGUERITE. Oh, no...I *couldn't.*

JESSIE. Why not?

MARGUERITE. I just *couldn't! (Pause.)* Who would be so hateful as to bomb a church?

JESSIE. I don't know.

MARGUERITE. Don't tell me.

JESSIE *(furious).* Now you see?

MARGUERITE. Don't be mad at me, don't be mad at me.

JESSIE. You want a Co-Cola?

MARGUERITE. Yes, please. *(JESSIE goes into house.)* You're the only one I know does wash on Sundays.

JESSIE (*off*). It's how I pray.

MARGUERITE. I don't feel well. (*She remembers she's alone; calling.*) Jessie? I don't feel well!

(*JESSIE reenters with Cokes. They sit primly, imitating rich women's tea parties.*)

JESSIE. What's the matter with you?

MARGUERITE. Thank you.

JESSIE. You're welcome.

MARGUERITE. Heart.

JESSIE. You're too young.

MARGUERITE. Feel. (*JESSIE feels MARGUERITE's heart.*)

JESSIE. Lay off that Co-Cola.

MARGUERITE. Can't. I'm hooked.

JESSIE. You are not!

MARGUERITE. I am.

JESSIE. Make yourself some snakeroot tea. That'll cure ya.

MARGUERITE. Don't wanna be cured. Only thing that makes me feel good.

JESSIE (*rises*). I don't wanna talk personal right now.

MARGUERITE. Then I'll just go over to Lily Meyers'. She'll talk to me.

JESSIE. She'll talk to anybody.

MARGUERITE. Nate Meyers is never home.

JESSIE. How 'bout that?

MARGUERITE. She says that's what keeps 'em together.

JESSIE. Isn't that awful?

MARGUERITE. It's the Club keeps Tom and me together.

JESSIE. What they got ta do with it?

MARGUERITE. He didn't have anybody to protect they wouldn'ta let him in.

JESSIE. That's not the only reason he stays with you.

MARGUERITE. Who knows *why* they do things. *(She checks her heart.)*

JESSIE. Better?

MARGUERITE. Worse.

JESSIE. Maybe you're upset.

MARGUERITE. Maybe.

JESSIE. Sometimes it's hard to tell.

MARGUERITE. What keeps you and Ed together?

JESSIE. We're married. *(Pause.)*

MARGUERITE. I was up 'til four this morning.

JESSIE. I was too. You shoulda called me.

MARGUERITE. You wouldn'ta answered.

JESSIE. Sometimes I don't feel like talkin'.

MARGUERITE. Then how'm I s'posed to get through?

JESSIE. Ring twice. I'll call you back.

MARGUERITE. Then you'll know it's me and you won't.

JESSIE. What were you doin' up so late?

MARGUERITE. Watchin' Betty Connor walk her dog.

JESSIE. Where was Albert?

MARGUERITE *(innocently)*. Where was Ed?

JESSIE *(spitefully)*. Where was Tom?

MARGUERITE. Albert Junior got arrested for drugs, you know.

JESSIE. How'd you find out?

MARGUERITE. Not Betty. She won't talk to me.

JESSIE. Maybe she didn't want anybody to know.

MARGUERITE. Always helps to talk to somebody.

JESSIE. Not always.

MARGUERITE. She tell you? *(JESSIE shrugs.)* Tell you how Little Albert got caught? Big Albert turned him in. T'teach him a lesson. Only it backfired on all of 'em. He's gonna be away a lot longer than any of 'em thought, especially Betty. *(Pause.)* You heard from *your* kids?

JESSIE. No.

MARGUERITE. I figured you'da told me if you did.

JESSIE. Oh yes.

MARGUERITE. I'll let you know if I hear anythin'.

JESSIE. You do that.

MARGUERITE. I will.

JESSIE. Fine. *(Pause.)*

MARGUERITE. It'd scare me to death if *I* didn't know where *my* kids were.

JESSIE. Least they got out.

MARGUERITE. What?

JESSIE. Doesn't scare me.

MARGUERITE. Even with Ed outa work all the time and gone so much?...

JESSIE. Hearin' it from you is worse than livin' through it! *(Pause.)*

MARGUERITE. Whenever Tom goes off all night, I just imagine he's dead. I got his funeral all picked out.

JESSIE. They cost a lot of money.

MARGUERITE. It's a cloudy day. We're all up on a hill. All our friends are there. I'm wearin' a simple black dress with a princess waist that I bought with his final pay. Everybody looks at me and knows how much I loved that man. I don't hear a word the preacher says. I break down and throw myself onto the coffin, and all his old girlfriends wish they'd been me. It's the most important day of my life. *(Pause.)* I am sure not feelin' well.

JESSIE. Go and see a doctor.

MARGUERITE. I wouldn't bother no doctor on a Sunday!

JESSIE. That's what he's for!

MARGUERITE. No, I think I'll just go lie down for a while.

JESSIE. That's the silliest thing I ever heard! Just call a doctor!

MARGUERITE. I don't want no doctor thinkin' I'm stupid!

JESSIE. Then quit that Co-Cola!

MARGUERITE. That's not what's wrong with me!

JESSIE. Well, then...

MARGUERITE. What if somebody was hurt in that church? *(They look at each other.)* We shoulda prayed. I got instincts. I just don't listen to 'em. They come to my head but not to the resta me. *(She falls to the ground and clasps her hands together fervently.)* I pray nobody got hurt in that exploded church.

JESSIE. I pray that too.

MARGUERITE. There's still time to take it back, Lord. We haven't heard it on the news yet.

JESSIE. Hallelujah!

MARGUERITE. I pray winter comes cold and keeps everybody inside.

JESSIE. That's right!

MARGUERITE. I pray for lower taxes and a brand new car and I pray you hear me prayin', Lord, 'cause I can't get what I want! I just can't! I don't know how! You get it for me! OK? Amen! *(She rises and dusts herself off.)* Now we got to sacrifice somethin'.

ED *(from inside house)*. Jessie!

MARGUERITE. Damn!

ED *(off)*. Jessie!

JESSIE. Out here!

(They hurry to clothesline, rip down two sheets and hang them up together as ED enters.)

ED *(unwelcomingly)*. Marguerite.

MARGUERITE. Ed. How ya doin'?

ED. Tom's home.

MARGUERITE. He *is?*

ED. Just saw him.

MARGUERITE. I didn't know *when* he'd be back.

ED. Back now.

MARGUERITE. Isn't that nice?

ED. I'm hungry. *(Pause.)* I'm hungry.

JESSIE. There's bologna in the icebox.

ED. Don't want bologna.

JESSIE. When I finish here I'll make you some lunch.

ED. Forget it.

JESSIE. Just give me a minute.

ED. Not hungry anymore. *(He stands there glaring at them a minute, then goes upstage, picks a blade of grass and brings it to JESSIE, holds it up to her face.)* See this?

JESSIE. Uh-huh.

ED. Grew.

JESSIE. Uh-huh.

ED. You said it wouldn't.

JESSIE. Did I say that?

ED. Uh-huh.

JESSIE. I thought it'd need some tendin' to is all.

ED. Didn't.

JESSIE. No.

ED. Grew.

JESSIE. Did I say it wouldn't?

ED. Well, I didn't.

JESSIE. Uh-huh.

ED. Don't never bet against grass. *(He keeps holding it in front of her face.)*

MARGUERITE. Well, I better get back before the phone rings and I'm not there.

JESSIE. I guess you better.

MARGUERITE. I am. *(MARGUERITE exits to alley; ED drops blade of grass, exits into house; JESSIE pulls the wash down, rehangs it.)*

JESSIE. I was born in a small town in the South. Mount Olive. You never heard of it. I knew I was destined... Often, as a child, I pictured myself in the pictures, portrayin' a woman who wanted to get into pictures...who got recognized by everybody for which she got a million dollars and never hadta worry again...I didn't get my start 'til I left home and moved to the city, where I was discovered bein' a female at a cash register...I married the man who discovered me...and now I look back and I wonder, what happened to all those girls I knew who wanted what I got. How come they didn't make it and I did? Why me?

(A shadow of light streaks by on the periphery; when JESSIE tries to look at it, it disappears. ED reenters with a beer.)

ED. Who you talkin' to?

JESSIE. Just myself. *(ED looks around suspiciously.)* People been callin' here all mornin'.

ED. Who?

JESSIE. I don't know. Didn't answer.

ED. How come?

JESSIE. Just didn't feel like talkin' today.

ED. That's all you been doin'.

JESSIE. But I didn't want to! Just happened!

ED. I was expectin' a call!

JESSIE. Now you're home, you can answer.

ED. You hear the news?

JESSIE. You know I get distressed when I hear news. I get a buzz in my ears. Hafta sit down. Can't think. Can't do anythin'. Makes me sit at the winda, lookin' out. Watchin' for the mailman if it's not a Sunday, comin' closer and closer, stoppin' at every house like he was feedin' it 'til he gets to ours and slams the box lid down on the bills and then fades away like music...or that street cleaner comin' around, you know, with that screamin' machine that eats whatever gets in its way, kittens and gym shoes, and all the little children run out of their houses screamin' and cryin' to save the lives of their toys, rushin' in fronta the street machine and grabbin' what they can before it runs 'em over, roarin' by as slow...as slow as a useless life...

ED. Somebody bombed a colored church...(*Pause.*) Blew the bottom out of it. Wish I'da seen it. (*He stands watching her work.*)

JESSIE. Who would do such a terrible, terrible thing as that?

ED. Somebody knew somethin' we didn't, I guess. (*Pause; JESSIE continues working.*)

JESSIE. Was anybody hurt?

ED. Only way some people learn.

JESSIE. Wouldn't it be awful if somebody was hurt?

ED. Have you ever wanted for a thing? (*Furiously, ED exits into house; JESSIE turns, at a loss.*)

JESSIE. You...you want lunch? You want lunch? Ed? You hear me? You want lunch?

(*ED reappears with a bundle: a set of filthy work clothes just like the ones he has on.*)

ED. I gotta have these for work tomorrow. (*He hands them to her, goes inside. JESSIE stares at them, then quickly searches the pockets, keeping an eye out for his return.*)

JESSIE. What did you get on these?...Ed?...Ed!...I don't think this is gonna come out...What did you get on these?

(Absorbed, JESSIE doesn't see ED reenter.)

JESSIE. This isn't gonna come out...this isn't gonna come out!

ED. Just dirt.

JESSIE *(jumps)*. Not just dirt.

ED. Alabama dirt. *(They stare at each other; he pulls a wad of bills from his pocket.)* Here. *(Hands her one.)*

JESSIE. Where...where'd this come from?

ED. Got paid. *(Pause; ED heads out through the alley.)*

JESSIE. Where you goin' now?

ED. One little bomb goes off and the whole town explodes. I gotta see that.

JESSIE. Supper's at seven.

ED. Too bad.

JESSIE. Why?

ED. Won't be here.

JESSIE. You won't be home for Sunday supper?

ED. Don't feel like it.

JESSIE. We always have Sunday supper!

ED. Look at you.

JESSIE. What's wrong?

ED. You fall for it every time.

JESSIE. I don't feel well.

ED. Look OK.

JESSIE. Got a funny feelin' in my chest.

ED. Don't call no doctor.

JESSIE. Lord, no, I'd never call a doctor on a Sunday.

ED. Can't afford no doctor.

JESSIE. It's just a little thing. Too much Co-Cola. Coke always makes me nervous. I been nervous all day.

ED. Don't drink my likker.

JESSIE. I won't.

ED. Don't be nervous, neither. Don't want my wife nervous.

JESSIE. I don't mind bein' nervous once in a while.

ED. You tryin' to kill me?

JESSIE. No!

ED. Feels like it!

JESSIE. I worry.

ED. See there!

JESSIE. I'm afraid!

ED. What'd I tell ya?

JESSIE. What'd I do?

ED. You think I don't know what I'm doin'.

JESSIE. I don't think I think that.

ED. How'm I s'posed to do anythin' knowin' they's people in the world thinkin' I can't?

JESSIE. They just don't know you.

ED. That's right. People don't even know me are thinkin' I'm nothin' right now. Thinkin' less than that. Not thinkin' about me at all. Puttin' their thoughts up all over the country so's I can't get around them. I'm trapped in their brains. I'm trapped. I ain't ever gonna get out. And you just like them.

JESSIE. I didn't mean to hurt your feelin's.

ED. I accept what I am. You see me marchin' over Red Mountain through the rich people's neighborhood, just to prove I'm equal as them? No, you don't. I admit myself. I accept what I am. Don't I? Don't I?

JESSIE. Yes, you do. (She goes to him, touches his back.)

ED. It's them that don't accept. They over the mountain in they livin' rooms. Talkin' 'bout rights at cocktail parties. Holdin' they fingers out from the glass. No colored movin' into their neighborhoods. Movin' into ours. We white as them. White as them. Come we don't get nothin' for it?

JESSIE. Maybe we done somethin' wrong.

ED. I didn't do nothin'. 'Cept get born.

JESSIE. You sure?

ED. You don't know who you're livin' with. You don't know who I am.

JESSIE. I don't wanna know.

ED. That's my girl. *(ED leaves quietly while her back is turned.)*

JESSIE. Don't go...Please, don't go...Ed? *(She turns.)* Ed?... Where'd you go?...*(JESSIE turns back to the line, pulls down laundry and rehangs it. The shadow of light streaks across the yard; JESSIE turns to look at it and it's gone; she returns uneasily to her work.)* I became famous so's I'd always be in the papers and my children would know where I was if they needed me...I know they'd come home if they could...but I gave 'em too much TV when they was growin' up and they think people were made just to entertain 'em. Me, I'm too real for them to come and see...I'm very real. *(Pause.)*

BIG ALBERT *(from inside house).* Ed?...ED!...*(JESSIE looks wildly around, wanting to escape; steps in a few directions, stops, trapped.)* ED!

(BIG ALBERT and BETTY appear from house; they're dressed for church; BIG ALBERT carries a Bible.)

JESSIE. NO!

BIG ALBERT. Jessie?

JESSIE. Yes!

BIG ALBERT. Ed around?

JESSIE. No!

BIG ALBERT. You know where he went?

JESSIE. No! Yes! Downtown! Just left! *(BETTY hangs back, staring at JESSIE.)*

BIG ALBERT. Shouldn't leave the house open like that when he's not around.

JESSIE. I never lock my door.

BIG ALBERT. Well, now you better.

JESSIE. They need to be locked, Ed does it.

BIG ALBERT. Didn't you hear the news this mornin'?

JESSIE. News? What news?

BIG ALBERT. Somebody bombed a colored church.

JESSIE (*feigning shock*). What?

BIG ALBERT. You heard me.

JESSIE. A church?

BIG ALBERT. That's where they gather.

JESSIE. Good Lord, who in the world would do such a terrible thing as that?

BIG ALBERT. Well, we got a war goin' on here now.

JESSIE. Not me. I don't!

BIG ALBERT. You a part of the country.

JESSIE. Not a part of no war.

BIG ALBERT. Well, you are, whether you like it or not. You an American. (*Pause.*)

JESSIE. Was anybody hurt, Albert? Nobody was hurt in that church, were they?

BIG ALBERT. It's a war, Jessie. (*BETTY, behind BIG ALBERT, nods; gestures wildly, indicating four little girls. JESSIE turns away, trips and falls; BETTY starts after her, checks herself and stops; JESSIE picks herself up.*)

JESSIE. I fell!

BIG ALBERT. You all right there?

JESSIE. I hurt my hand!

BETTY. She's all right.

JESSIE. What?

BETTY. You're all right.

JESSIE. I'm all right! I'm all right!

BIG ALBERT. I gotta catch up with Ed.

JESSIE. Can Betty stay, Albert? You wanta Co-Cola? Wanta cookie? How's Little Albert?

BIG ALBERT. In jail.

JESSIE. Jail! Oh! I'm so sorry!

BIG ALBERT. She sneaks off to see him when I'm not around. She thinks I won't find out. She knows how he is. I won't see him.

JESSIE. Your own son?

BIG ALBERT. I saw him right now I'd kill him with my bare hands.

JESSIE. You don't mean that!

BIG ALBERT. I gave him to the government. I couldn't do anythin' with him. They know what to do. They'll straighten him out.

JESSIE. Lotta colored in that jail!

BIG ALBERT. He's gonna act like them he's gonna hafta be with them.

JESSIE. Oh, Albert, I hope nobody bombs the jail!

BIG ALBERT. They're the ones we got the jail *for,* honey. Nobody in their right mind'd blow up a jail.

JESSIE. God might!

BIG ALBERT. Who you been talkin' to, honey?

JESSIE. Just myself.

BIG ALBERT. Watch who you talk to, Jessie. You don't know who anybody is in a war. Betty! (*He moves toward the house.*)

BETTY (*confidentially*). You all right? (*BIG ALBERT turns, watching them; JESSIE sees this.*)

JESSIE. I got a funny feelin' in my chest.

BETTY (*playing along*). Albert gets that!

JESSIE (*to BIG ALBERT*). You do?

BIG ALBERT. Climbin' stairs. You get it climbin' stairs?

JESSIE. I don't know. We don't got any.

BIG ALBERT. Try climbin' stairs.

JESSIE. I'll go find some.

BIG ALBERT. You know what it is?

JESSIE. No.

BIG ALBERT. One of these days I'll get to a doctor.

JESSIE. Well, I hope you do, Albert.

BIG ALBERT. Oh, I will. Soon as Betty makes me. Sure you're all right?

JESSIE (*shaking*). I'm always all right.

BIG ALBERT. You should come over and talk to Betty. She's always sick.

JESSIE. I will.

BETTY. When?

JESSIE. I...(*Suddenly, she's lost.*)

BIG ALBERT. What's the matter now?

BETTY. She's all right.

BIG ALBERT. Don't look all right to me.

JESSIE. I depend so on the weather as to how I feel. Sky clouds up and I get dizzy. What's it doin' up there today? I can't think.

BIG ALBERT. I'll tell you what to think.

JESSIE. I wish somebody would.

BIG ALBERT. Lock up.

JESSIE. Yes, Albert.

BETTY. Bye-bye. (*BIG ALBERT pulls BETTY off; JESSIE pulls the wash down again.*)

JESSIE. This...is my lovely estate...Just a little place I bought...to get away...from bein' famous...I...decorated it...in white...I have white everythin'...white furniture...white carpetin'...white walls...white...bed linen...I do all the cleanin' myself...nobody else touches my house...I never realized how much white shows up the dirt...I clean from top to bottom every day...It's how I pray. *(She comes to the end of the wash; stands at a loss with the sheets cradled in her arms. The shadow of light appears; disappears; JESSIE does not look at it.)*

SCENE THREE

AT RISE: *Monday morning. JESSIE hangs the same laundry she took down in Scene Two. MARGUERITE enters from the alley; she carries an empty coffee cup as a pretext for her visit. JESSIE sees her, avoids her. Both are extremely upset inside.*

MARGUERITE *(after the avoidance game has lasted long enough)*. WHY IN HELL DON'T YOU GET HIM TO BUY YOU A DRYER?!!

JESSIE *(furiously)*. WHO HAS MONEY LIKE THAT?

MARGUERITE. YOU JUST KEEP DOIN' THE SAME LAUNDRY OVER AND OVER AGAIN!

JESSIE. GOT DIRTY AGAIN! *(They retreat. JESSIE works harder; MARGUERITE slumps onto a tub, exhausted, staring; JESSIE eyes her warily.)*

MARGUERITE. Can I have a cup of Co-Cola and a donut? *(JESSIE stops and stares at her; she stares back.)* Please? *(JESSIE drops what she's doing and heads inside.)* Thank you!

JESSIE *(angrily, as she exits)*. You're welcome! *(Pause. JESSIE returns with a bottle of Coke, donut and napkin on a plate.)*

MARGUERITE. Oh, I better not after all. I'm on a diet. *(JESSIE turns and goes toward house.)* Wait! Wait! *(JESSIE brings food back to her.)* I shouldn't. *(She takes it.)* Thank you…*(Overbearingly.) Thank you!*

JESSIE. You're *welcome! (JESSIE goes back to work with a vengeance. MARGUERITE pours Coke into her cup, dips her donut into it and eats.)*

MARGUERITE *(sighing).* I am a victim of this food.

JESSIE. You can stop yourself.

MARGUERITE. Oh no. I can't. You don't mind if I just sit here for a while, do you, Jessie?

JESSIE. I don't mind. *(She does.)*

MARGUERITE. Whole town's gone up, Jessie. That's what they say.

JESSIE. Can't feel it from the outskirts.

MARGUERITE. Two white boys went and shot some little colored boy ridin' on the handlebars of his brother's bike. Children, Jessie. Can't go downtown. The army's there. Colored everywhere, throwin' rocks and pullin' people outa their cars.

JESSIE. That so?

MARGUERITE. They's colored livin' just a block from here. They gonna come and get us. They know we alone in our house all day. They know where we are. White people shine like new dimes in the sun. All the trees on this block are dead. They's no shade left anywheres around here. We're exposed!

JESSIE. It's the season.

MARGUERITE. You can't tell death from change! *(The phone rings once; they turn toward house.)*

JESSIE *(pretending to shrug it off).* That's funny.

MARGUERITE *(turns back from house uneasily).* I started smokin'. Look. *(She takes a cigarette out of her pocket and lights it, trembling.)*

JESSIE. When did you start that?

MARGUERITE. Last night.

JESSIE. Well, for goodness sake, quit!

MARGUERITE. I can't! I'm hooked!

JESSIE. Costs money to smoke!

MARGUERITE. I don't care about the money.

JESSIE. Marguerite!

MARGUERITE. I tried callin' you last night! *(Pause.)*

JESSIE. You did?

MARGUERITE. You knew it was me!

JESSIE. I couldn't talk!

MARGUERITE. You heard about them little girls! Them poor little girls! How their mamas ever gonna live without them? *(JESSIE spits on MARGUERITE; MARGUERITE screeches, wipes it off and spits back; they do this a few times.)*

BETTY *(off).* Jessie!

(BETTY appears from house; she carries a catalog as a pretext.)

MARGUERITE *(jumps, halts, turns).* Betty!

BETTY *(disappointed).* Marguerite!

MARGUERITE. Hello, stranger!

BETTY. Are you here?

MARGUERITE. We're visitin'!

BETTY. I didn't mean to interrupt. I'll catch you later.

JESSIE. You didn't interrupt.

BETTY *(making eye contact).* Oh yes, I did.

JESSIE. No, you didn't.

BETTY *(pointedly)* You didn't notice. I'll come back later.

JESSIE. We want you to stay!

BETTY. No, you don't!

MARGUERITE *(lying).* Well, of course we do.

BETTY. You wanted me to stay I'da been invited!

MARGUERITE. We never know what we want!

BETTY. You don't know what *I* want!

MARGUERITE. Sit down, dammit!

JESSIE. Marguerite!

MARGUERITE. I get so sick of her lack of confidence!

BETTY. Well, just for one minute. *(The phone rings once; she panics for JESSIE.)* That's funny!

JESSIE *(quickly)*. Would you care for a Co-Cola!

MARGUERITE. I'm havin' one!

BETTY. I would love a Co-Cola! *(JESSIE goes inside; BETTY follows after her; MARGUERITE follows BETTY; BETTY halts.)*

MARGUERITE. How have you been, Betty?

BETTY. How have *you* been?

MARGUERITE. Oh, fine, just fine.

BETTY. That's how I been too.

MARGUERITE. What you got there?

(JESSIE reenters with Coke.)

BETTY. What?

MARGUERITE. That right there!

BETTY. Oh! It's…it's the new catalog from Penney's. *(MARGUERITE squeals with delight and tries to grab the catalog from BETTY, who holds onto it.)* Well, don't tear it now!

MARGUERITE. Don't take it away don't take it away don't take it away! *(BETTY pulls the catalog away and sits down with it; MARGUERITE and JESSIE crowd around her. With ceremony, BETTY opens the catalog; JESSIE hands her the Coke.)*

BETTY. Thank you.

JESSIE. You're welcome.

BETTY. Will you look at that? *(They stare down at open page; MARGUERITE starts to weep.)*

JESSIE. It's all right, Marguerite. Shhhh, honey. Shh...

MARGUERITE. Why don't I look like that?

BETTY. You just don't.

MARGUERITE. But I want to!

BETTY. There's just some things you'll never be able to do in life.

JESSIE. Turn the page! Turn the page!

MARGUERITE. She's everywhere!

BETTY. It's not your fault.

MARGUERITE. Yes, it is.

JESSIE. We love the way you look.

MARGUERITE. I don't care what *you* think! I care 'bout everybody else!

BETTY. She's probably stupid.

MARGUERITE. That's the real me. I looked like that, you'd see me!

BETTY. Get Tom to buy that dress for you!

MARGUERITE. I need that dress! I need it!

JESSIE. 'Course you do.

BETTY. I let Albert see the real me once.

MARGUERITE. What'd he do?

BETTY. Laughed.

MARGUERITE *(in horror)*. Why?

BETTY *(deadpan)*. I must be funny.

MARGUERITE *(righteously)*. How could you stay with him after that?

BETTY. Jessie, could you put a little somethin' hard in this soda?

JESSIE. It's eleven in the mornin'!

BETTY (*meaningfully*). It's flat. (*JESSIE takes Coke, heads inside.*) Wait up, I'll help you! (*BETTY rises; MARGUE-RITE holds her back.*)

MARGUERITE. Stay here and tell me how you really been.

BETTY. I did already.

MARGUERITE. I haven't seen you in ages.

BETTY. You're not my husband. (*She pulls away from MAR-GUERITE.*)

MARGUERITE. What you got to talk to Jessie about?

BETTY. None a your business!

MARGUERITE. I don't keep secrets in fronta you!

BETTY. I don't talk to you anymore!

MARGUERITE. And I forgive you. I'd never keep a secret away from you. No matter whose it was, I'd tell you.

BETTY. It's a secret!

MARGUERITE. What makes you think I need to know?

BETTY. I'm sorry, Marguerite.

MARGUERITE. She'll just tell me when you leave.

BETTY. Jessie keeps secrets.

MARGUERITE. Not from me, she doesn't.

BETTY. Oh yes, she does.

MARGUERITE. Oh no, she doesn't.

BETTY. Then what's she told you?

MARGUERITE. It's our secret.

(*JESSIE comes out with liquor bottle as BETTY turns to go in.*)

BETTY. I wanted to help you!

MARGUERITE. I couldn't wait.

BIG ALBERT (*from inside house*). Jessie!...Jessie!

BETTY. What's *he* doin' home? (*In terror she runs off into alley.*)

JESSIE. Here we are, Albert!

(BIG ALBERT appears.)

BIG ALBERT *(distressed)*. Mornin'.

JESSIE. Mornin'.

MARGUERITE. Mornin', Albert.

BIG ALBERT. Betty over here?

JESSIE. Why, no. We haven't seen her.

MARGUERITE. You lose your job, Albert?

JESSIE. Marguerite! What an awful thing to say!

BIG ALBERT. Ain't no work. Town's gone crazy! You seen Betty?

MARGUERITE. Betty won't talk to me anymore.

BIG ALBERT. Go home, Marguerite. And don't let nobody see you.

MARGUERITE. Is ever'thin' all right, Albert?

BIG ALBERT. What I tell you about leavin' your door open?

JESSIE. I forgot!

BIG ALBERT. She left our door open too.

JESSIE. I'm so sorry.

MARGUERITE. I bet Betty's sorry too. I hope nothin' happened to her. Now I'm gonna worry.

BIG ALBERT. You see her, tell her to get her ass to home and go the back way. Got that?

MARGUERITE. Get her ass to home and go the back way.

JESSIE. What's wrong?

BIG ALBERT *(seeing the bottle)*. You girls're startin' a little early, ain't ya?

MARGUERITE. We're celebratin'.

BIG ALBERT. What?

MARGUERITE. Tom's gonna buy me this new dress. *(She shows BIG ALBERT the catalog; he snorts.)* What's so funny?

BIG ALBERT. Don't change. *(He exits through house.)*

JESSIE *(loudly).* I'll show you out, Albert!

(JESSIE sets bottle down, follows BIG ALBERT off. BETTY sneaks back in, grabs bottle and pours more liquor into her cup; JESSIE comes back; she and MARGUERITE stare at BETTY.)

BETTY. Oh, don't look at me thataway. I haven't become a alcoholic or anythin'. What's a alcoholic, anyway? Somebody who feels better when they drink. We're all alcoholics.

MARGUERITE. Not me, of course.

BETTY. You need that dress. You need it!

MARGUERITE. No dress is gonna cloud my eyes and make me drive into a telephone pole.

BETTY. It's slow-actin'. Might take years for your wardrobe to accumulate in your bloodstream! Then one day, whammo! O.D.!

JESSIE. Where'd you pick that up?

BETTY. What?

JESSIE. "O.D."

BETTY. Those kinda words taken over my house.

MARGUERITE. I o.d.'d once...on Rolaids...hadta have my stomach pumped.

BETTY. I took the bus to Little Albert this mornin'.

JESSIE. You did!

MARGUERITE. How is he?

BETTY. I figured he'd be wastin' away, scared and lonely and ready to repent. I hoped it. But all he is, is more like he was. Only person in the family that's scared is me. I'm the only one lonely. Only one repentant. How come he never wanted to be like me?

MARGUERITE. TV says they gonna be able to do that some day soon. Take a little piece of you and grow you another you exactly like yourself. Then I guess you can give yourself everythin' you never had and see if it makes you any better.

JESSIE. They let you bring Little Albert things?

BETTY. He says they just get stolen.

MARGUERITE. He's with a lot who know howta do that.

BETTY. The guards take it.

MARGUERITE. Well, now, I don't believe that.

BETTY. Then don't.

MARGUERITE. We woulda heard about it if it were true.

BETTY. No time in the news for somethin' like that with all the car wrecks and Kennedys and marchin' and g.d. conflicts in some weird-soundin' place nobody can pronounce. *(She takes a card out of her pocket and writes on it as she talks, discreetly.)*

MARGUERITE. Vieet-Nam.

BETTY. I *know.*

JESSIE. Where is Vieet-Nam?

MARGUERITE. Africa.

BETTY. Good!

JESSIE. Africa! What're we doin' there?

MARGUERITE. Hellin' around as usual.

BETTY. Gettin' away from the wives. *(Pause; she goes to JESSIE.)* Here's that recipe I promised. *(She gives JESSIE the card.)*

JESSIE *(staring at card, shocked)*. Ed?

MARGUERITE. What?

BETTY *(furiously)*. What?

JESSIE *(innocently)*. What? *(She turns away, stricken.)*

MARGUERITE. What's wrong with Jessie?

BETTY. Nothin'.

MARGUERITE. Can I see?

BETTY. It's not for you.

MARGUERITE. What's wrong with me?

BETTY. It's just for Jessie.

MARGUERITE. I know what it is.

BETTY. You do not!

MARGUERITE. Yes, I do!

BETTY. Not if you know what's good for you!

MARGUERITE. Then tell me, else I'll sic my intuition on you! *(Pause.)*

BETTY. It's my secret recipe for white bread!

MARGUERITE. I knew it!

BETTY. It's still secret! *(JESSIE begins to weep.)* Isn't it, Jessie? *(JESSIE nods, overcome.)*

MARGUERITE. Well, it's not that big a deal!

BETTY *(making it up as she goes)*. That recipe come across the ocean with my great-great-grandmother! She brought it from the deserts of France where the women gathered once a year in the caves and took off alla their clothes and danced together 'til the Virgin Mary appeared and talked to them in a tongue they'd never heard before but still understood.

MARGUERITE. What she say? What she say?

BETTY. Girls, she said, don't never go inta politics. Politics is just a buncha rules we make up so's we don't hafta face ourselves and change. Girls, she said, they's a whole 'nother world in the world. A whole 'nother world! Then she blew her nose in a maple leaf even though there weren't no maples in France and said she weren't no virgin!

JESSIE. Oh, my! *(JESSIE and BETTY start to laugh.)*

MARGUERITE *(disappointed)*. She wasn't?

BETTY. She just didn't want kids!

(Pause; JESSIE and BETTY scream with laughter. BIG ALBERT appears at house door.)

BIG ALBERT. KNEW YOU WERE HERE! *(The WOMEN gasp and jump.)*

MARGUERITE. Jesus wept, Albert! You just walk in anybody's house?

BIG ALBERT. Anybody dumb enough to leave their front door open!

JESSIE. I'll go lock it right now!

BIG ALBERT. Too late! *(to BETTY.)* You been over here this whole time?

BETTY. No, Albert.

MARGUERITE. We told her you come by.

BETTY. I was so worried. I thought you'd lost your job.

BIG ALBERT. Time to go home, now.

BETTY. All right. *(To WOMEN.)* He takes good care of me.

MARGUERITE. Aw, does she hafta go?

BIG ALBERT. Tom's callin', Marguerite.

MARGUERITE. Tom's at work.

BIG ALBERT. Not anymore.

JESSIE. Where's Ed?

BIG ALBERT. Come on, Betty.

JESSIE. Albert? Is Ed comin' home too?

BIG ALBERT. Don't you worry 'bout Ed, now.

JESSIE *(worried)*. Where is he?

BIG ALBERT. You just sit right there.

JESSIE. Should I do somethin'?

BIG ALBERT. Don't do nothin'! *(He and BETTY exit.)*

MARGUERITE. I'll go ask Tom if you should do somethin'.

JESSIE. You do that.

MARGUERITE. I will. *(She hurries off; JESSIE cleans up.)*

JESSIE. Yes, I know Jack and Jackie...I'm over to the White House all the time...What are they really like?...They're poor white trash. Just poor white trash that made it...Why do you want to know about them? Why don't you want to know about me?

(JESSIE goes to line, pulls down wash; the shadow of light appears; JESSIE stiffens, aware of it, does not look; it remains until MARGUERITE barges in.)

MARGUERITE. Tom says I can't come over here anymore!

JESSIE. Why?

MARGUERITE. Tom says—

(BIG ALBERT enters from the alley.)

BIG ALBERT. Didn't I tell you to go home?

MARGUERITE. I did!

BIG ALBERT. Don't get yourself seen comin' over here!

MARGUERITE. Tom told me already.

BIG ALBERT. Then you shoulda listened.

JESSIE. You better listen to him, Marguerite.

MARGUERITE. I did!

BIG ALBERT. All right, now, Jessie, don't get nervous or nothin'.

JESSIE. Yes, Albert.

BIG ALBERT. Nothin' to get nervous about. Everythin''s gonna be fine.

JESSIE. Yes, Albert. What is?

BIG ALBERT *(to MARGUERITE)*. Didn't you tell her?

MARGUERITE. Tom told me not to!

BIG ALBERT. P'lice picked up Ed about an hour ago.

JESSIE *(stunned)*. What for?

BIG ALBERT. Say he's the one bombed that colored church.

JESSIE. Oh no! Oh no! Oh no! Oh no!

BIG ALBERT. Now calm down.

JESSIE. Ed? My Ed?

BIG ALBERT. Easy, honey, easy.

JESSIE. Where is he? Is he all right? Where is he, Albert?

BIG ALBERT. They got him down to Birmingham jail.

JESSIE. Well, I'm gonna go there right now.

BIG ALBERT. They not gonna let you see him.

JESSIE. He's *my* husband!

BIG ALBERT. Gonna hafta wait a little while.

JESSIE. Ain't they gonna let him out on whattayacallit?

BIG ALBERT. You don't have that kind of money.

JESSIE. What'm I gonna do? What'm I gonna do?

BIG ALBERT. Can't do nothin'.

JESSIE. He's safe, though, ain't he? He's safe, that's all I
    wanta know.

BIG ALBERT. Makes you think he's safe?

JESSIE. He's in the jail.

BIG ALBERT. You put your faith in the government?

JESSIE. I'm an American!

BIG ALBERT. You fall for that?

JESSIE. You do!

BIG ALBERT. Not me!

JESSIE. What about Little Albert?

BIG ALBERT. I know some things you don't.

JESSIE. Tell me. What?

BIG ALBERT. You don't know, I'm not gonna tell ya. But
    you're stupid, you don't know.

JESSIE. Please, Albert.

BIG ALBERT. Ed didn't do nothin' wrong.

JESSIE. Then why'd they take my husband?

BIG ALBERT. Somebody broke the oath! *(Pause.)*

JESSIE. I don't understand.

BIG ALBERT. That's OK, honey. Half the p'lice force belongs to the Club. Whoever told on Ed, we gonna shut him up.

JESSIE. I wanta go shoppin'.

BIG ALBERT. What?

JESSIE. I...I *need* somethin'...

BIG ALBERT. You're not goin' shoppin'.

JESSIE. Feels so good just to buy.

BIG ALBERT. You hear what I said?

MARGUERITE. Won't hurt anybody she just goes shoppin'!

BIG ALBERT. She's not goin' anyplace!

JESSIE. You're not my husband.

MARGUERITE. Albert, you're makin' her upset!

JESSIE. I'm upset! I'm upset!

BIG ALBERT. Go home, Marguerite!

MARGUERITE. I am!

BIG ALBERT. Go home! You hear me?

MARGUERITE. Call me, Jessie!

BIG ALBERT. NOW!

MARGUERITE. I AM! *(She exits in a huff.)*

BIG ALBERT. Where you really goin'?

JESSIE. I just wanta *get* somethin' for a change, Albert.

BIG ALBERT. You seein' another man?

JESSIE *(stunned).* A man!

BIG ALBERT. You heard me.

JESSIE *(sincerely).* No other man'd want me!

BIG ALBERT. Maybe.

JESSIE. Look at my face! My poor poor face!

BIG ALBERT. Not about your face.

JESSIE. I'm not lookin' for no other man.

BIG ALBERT. Then who's gonna give you the money to go shoppin'?

JESSIE. Oh.

BIG ALBERT. Stay put. *(He starts to go, turns.)* Gonna get lonesome.

JESSIE. I got TV.

BIG ALBERT. We gonna be watchin' out for you.

JESSIE. Why, thank you, Albert.

BIG ALBERT. You do anythin' against Ed, anythin', we gonna come after you. You won't know when and you won't know why and you won't ever find out who we were. *(He exits.)*

JESSIE *(incredulously)*. No man'd want a woman like me. *(She gestures in grief and relief. Blackout.)*

END OF ACT ONE

ACT TWO

SCENE ONE

AT RISE: *November, 1963. Late evening. Brilliant red dresses now hang on the line. Beneath it, JESSIE lies sleeping, hidden under a pile of white sheets. She rises suddenly from the sheets like a phoenix, dressed in a white diaphanous nightgown. She freezes, crouches, hunts for something to eat off the ground; spies something, picks it up, bites into it, throws it down in disgust; goes to laundry pole and stretches against it luxuriously; turns and then straddles the pole, moves against it sensuously; begins to moan. As her moaning builds, MARGUERITE enters screaming. She is wearing a large overcoat to hide herself.*

MARGUERITE. Get in your house!

JESSIE. Marguerite! How nice to see you!

MARGUERITE *(looks around warily; takes JESSIE roughly by the arm and pulls her toward the house).* What in hell do you think you're doin' out here?

JESSIE. What?

MARGUERITE. I asked you!

JESSIE. I don't know.

MARGUERITE. You get inside your house, now, you hear? *(She deposits JESSIE at the back step.)* Go on! *(JESSIE stands, staring at her.)* Go on! *(JESSIE goes in obediently; turns in doorway and watches MARGUERITE.)* Now stay there! *(MARGUERITE starts to go off; JESSIE immediately*

41

comes out of her house and follows her; MARGUERITE whirls around.)

JESSIE. I got out!

MARGUERITE *(furiously)*. Get in your house! Get in your house! Get in your house and stay there!

JESSIE. You're not my husband!

MARGUERITE. I seen you out here!

JESSIE. You have?

MARGUERITE. So has everybody else!

JESSIE. Does my hair look all right?

MARGUERITE. I go to bed, I see you! I get up in the middle of the night, I see you! Everywhere I go in my house they's a view looks out on you, wanderin' around like a starvin' horse!

JESSIE. Maybe you shouldn't look.

MARGUERITE. I'm sick of you! I can't stand it anymore! You get inside right now, Jessie! Lock yourself in!

JESSIE. I can't.

MARGUERITE. Why won't you listen to me!

JESSIE. I don't sleep in the house anymore.

MARGUERITE. What's in there?

JESSIE *(evasively)*. Nobody.

MARGUERITE. They in there?

JESSIE *(fearfully)*. Who?

MARGUERITE. Your friends. Ones that give you all these dresses.

JESSIE. Ain't they pretty?

MARGUERITE. No! They're not!

JESSIE. Yes, they are!

MARGUERITE. You never had a red dress in your life! Where'd you get 'em?

JESSIE. They is the real me.

MARGUERITE. There ain't never been a real you! I don't even know who I'm talkin' to right now!

JESSIE. Maybe I'm happy. (*She digs the old shine bottle out of her nest of sheets, swigs from it.*)

MARGUERITE. You're not happy.

JESSIE. Well maybe this is what it looks like.

MARGUERITE. You're what happens to a woman left all alone.

JESSIE. You've just never seen me happy before.

MARGUERITE. You feel too much! That's what it is! It's makin' you crazy! Stop feelin'! Stop feelin'! Or you'll never be normal again!

JESSIE. All right, Marguerite.

MARGUERITE. Tell me what's goin' on over here, Jessie. I'm your friend.

JESSIE. I'm stickin' by my man.

MARGUERITE. Then who you got hidin' in your house?... They the police?

JESSIE. Oh, I don't think so.

MARGUERITE. The FBI? Tell me who they are! (*Pause.*)

JESSIE. Ghosts.

MARGUERITE. Ghosts!

JESSIE. The ghosts of animals, I think. Dogs mostly. Lotta dogs been through here lately. Hounds. They got red eyes. You can see the flash of their backs. Sometimes they seem wild. And sometimes they seem human, like innocent little children...They's lonesome, and hungry...but they never whine or beg...(*Pause.*)

MARGUERITE. They's comin'.

JESSIE. Who is?

MARGUERITE. You know who!

JESSIE. No!

MARGUERITE. I heard 'em!

JESSIE. Why?

MARGUERITE. That's what they's comin' to find out!

JESSIE. I've forgotten howta entertain!

MARGUERITE. That don't matter!

JESSIE. I don't remember howta talk to them!

MARGUERITE. They's comin' here to shut you up!

JESSIE. What'd I say?

MARGUERITE. Lock yourself in, Jessie!

JESSIE. I don't have a thing in the house.

MARGUERITE. Do what I tell you!

JESSIE. Ask them to come another time, Marguerite.

MARGUERITE. Hide yourself, you hear me? Put yourself away!

JESSIE. Tell 'em I got a headache!

MARGUERITE. They won't listen to me!

JESSIE. That one works every time.

MARGUERITE. Not this time!

JESSIE. You got to make them listen, Marguerite!

MARGUERITE. I don't gotta do nothin', you hear? I don't want them comin' after me! I got brains! Not like you!

JESSIE. Help me! *(She grabs hold of MARGUERITE desperately.)*

MARGUERITE. Lemme go!

JESSIE. Help me, Marguerite!

MARGUERITE. LET ME GO! *(She breaks JESSIE's hold and gets far away from her.)*

JESSIE. Don't let them get me! Stop them! Please!

MARGUERITE *(backing)*. I can't.

JESSIE. Please!

MARGUERITE. I can't!

JESSIE. PLEASE!

MARGUERITE. I can't! I can't! I can't! *(MARGUERITE runs off. The shadow of light appears; it stays in one place, very still and indistinct; JESSIE is still too, sensing it, not looking at it.)*

JESSIE *(to shadow).* You're not the only ones...they's all over Birmingham...Ghosts...white ghosts...Don't know what happened to 'em...Look starved...scared...always stay too long at the all-white lunch counters, always hauntin' the empty downtowns, hauntin' the 7-'Levens, tellin' cashiers their whole life's story so's they can stand a while in the air conditionin', 'round food... watchin' the streets outside that some of 'em built for a livin' before they got laid off, bucklin' in the heat...white ghosts...white ghost people...can't find the bodies they come from...no graves...they doomed to no relief...

(Suddenly, signal calls are heard; JESSIE looks around; they're heard again. She grabs her bottle, tears a red dress off the line and puts it on hurriedly as she hides behind some junk. The shadow of light disappears. TOM and BIG ALBERT enter. They wear makeshift Klan robes; they stalk the yard, wielding tire irons like sabers, hitting the ground at the slightest sound, pinning themselves to imaginary walls, SWAT-team-style. They discover JESSIE hiding; she emerges from her hiding place as if nothing were strange.)

JESSIE. Tom! Albert! How nice a you ta come!

BIG ALBERT. Who?

JESSIE. Who?

BIG ALBERT. Who you talkin' to?

JESSIE. Albert! Tom!

BIG ALBERT. That ain't me! *(They look at JESSIE; begin circling her.)* What you been doin' over here all alone?

TOM. Ain't got no money.

BIG ALBERT. How you live without money? (*JESSIE shrugs.*) Gonna starve soon.

TOM. Gonna starve.

BIG ALBERT. Gonna starve.

JESSIE. I'll get a job.

BIG ALBERT. Ain't no jobs!

TOM. How you gonna get a job?

BIG ALBERT. Nobody's gonna give you a job.

TOM. Nobody needs you.

BIG ALBERT. They gonna ask what all you done before.

TOM. Just like gettin' into heaven.

BIG ALBERT. Can't say nothin'.

TOM. That won't get you a job.

BIG ALBERT. They'll cut you off.

TOM. Cut you off at the future.

BIG ALBERT. They lookin' for a past.

TOM. You ain't got one.

BIG ALBERT. Everybody else needs a job too.

TOM. I need a job.

BIG ALBERT. I need a job!

TOM. Makes you think you're better than everybody else?

BIG ALBERT. Go and get a job right now.

TOM. Go on.

BIG ALBERT. Go on.

TOM. Go on.

BIG ALBERT. Go on.

TOM. Except don't move.

BIG ALBERT. Don't move.

TOM. Don't move.

JESSIE. Gets lonely here.

BIG ALBERT. Gets lonely.

TOM. Lonely.

BIG ALBERT. You so lonely how come you don't go to see your husband in jail?

TOM. Come you never went to his trial?

BIG ALBERT. Everybody's lookin' for you.

TOM. Everybody's askin'.

BIG ALBERT. Where you been, honey?

TOM. Where you been?

BIG ALBERT. Where you been?

JESSIE. I...tried to get there...

BIG ALBERT. She tried.

TOM. She tried.

JESSIE. I tried but I couldn't...I couldn't. I—

TOM. Couldn't get to your own husband's trial?

JESSIE (pause). THE CAR WOULDN'T START!

BIG ALBERT. What?

TOM. What?

BIG ALBERT. What?

TOM. What?

BIG ALBERT. What?

JESSIE. I tried everythin'! It wasn't outa gas! It wasn't outa tires or lights or nothin'! It just wouldn't start!

BIG ALBERT. She didn't take care of it!

TOM. Didn't take care of the car?

JESSIE. Nobody ever taught me how!

BIG ALBERT. She the one got taken care of!

TOM. She gets taken care of while all the resta us sit around rebuildin' our engines over and over and over again, and again and again and again and again, all the resta our lives, the resta our lives just repeatin' the same things, the same things, over and over and over again, and again and again and again and again, is that it?

BIG ALBERT. Who do you think you are, honey?

TOM. Who do you think you are? (Pause.)

BIG ALBERT. What?

TOM. What?

BIG ALBERT. What?

TOM. What? *(They've closed in on JESSIE; now they look at each other for confirmation.)* She forgot howta act!

BIG ALBERT. Know what happens to a woman who forgets how to act?

TOM. She gets put out!

BIG ALBERT. Out with the rapists and the robbers and the killers!

TOM. They waitin' for you!

BIG ALBERT. Waitin' in the shadows.

TOM. Waitin' in the alleys.

BIG ALBERT. Waitin' in the buses and the bars and the woods.

TOM. Know what they'll do to you?

JESSIE. Yes.

BIG ALBERT. What?

JESSIE. Yes!

TOM. No, you don't.

BIG ALBERT. You don't know.

TOM. Tell her.

BIG ALBERT. You tell her.

TOM. They'll slit your throat and rip your voice box out and leave it wrigglin' in the dirt like a newborn.

BIG ALBERT. These is modern times. *(They close in.)*

TOM. Not safe.

BIG ALBERT. Not safe.

TOM. Not safe.

BIG ALBERT. Not safe.

TOM. Hey, baby.

BIG ALBERT. Hey, baby. *(JESSIE cringes.)*

TOM. What'd I say?

BIG ALBERT. We didn't say nothin'. *(JESSIE gives up.)*

TOM. That's it.

BIG ALBERT. Now you got it. *(They move in.)*

TOM. Nice tits.

BIG ALBERT. Nice legs.

TOM. Nice lips.

BIG ALBERT. Nice hips.

(They grab JESSIE and she screams. BETTY and MAR-GUERITE run on from alley.)

BETTY. JESSIE! JESSIE! *(The WOMEN skid to a stop in mock surprise.)*

MARGUERITE. TOM?

BETTY. ALBERT? *(The MEN freeze.)*

JESSIE. Run, Betty! Run, Marguerite! That ain't Albert! That ain't Tom!

BETTY. What you doin'?

MARGUERITE. You cheatin' on us? *(The MEN drop JESSIE and turn on WOMEN in rage.)*

TOM. I could kill you right now! I could twist your head off like a light bulb and smash it on the ground! Don't you understand nothin'? Who do you think we are?

BIG ALBERT. You all right there, buddy? *(TOM seethes with rage; BETTY picks JESSIE up.)*

TOM. I'M BURNIN' UP! I'M BURNIN' UP!

BIG ALBERT. GET BACK! ALLA YOU! GET BACK!

TOM. I'M OUTA CONTROL! I'M GONNA KILL HER! I'M REALLY GONNA DO IT! WATCH ME! WATCH ME! YOU WATCHIN'? *(TOM lunges at MARGUERITE; BIG ALBERT grabs him as MARGUERITE steps back, appealing to him.)*

MARGUERITE. HELP ME!

TOM. HELP ME!

MARGUERITE. HELP ME!

BIG ALBERT. EASY BOY!

TOM. I'M GONNA BE SICK!

BIG ALBERT. HOLD ON NOW! *(TOM heaves in his arms; pants and shivers.)* Atta boy, you got it, you got it! Maybe you better sit down. You want to sit down? GET HIM A PLACE TO SIT DOWN! *(MARGUERITE rolls a tub to TOM; he collapses, weeping; BETTY holds JESSIE, who also weeps.)* You gonna be all right now, you gonna be all right. *(MARGUERITE stands too close, watching.)* STAY BACK! *(TOM swipes at MARGUERITE; she screams and runs to the other WOMEN; TOM tries to get loose from BIG ALBERT.)*

TOM. WE'RE NOT WHO YOU THINK WE ARE!

MARGUERITE. WE DIDN'T THINK ANYTHIN'!

TOM. WE'RE NOT WHO YOU DON'T THINK NEITHER!

BIG ALBERT. Keep your head on, boy.

TOM. NOBODY LISTENS!

BIG ALBERT. Boy needs somethin' ta drink. *(WOMEN stare at TOM.)* GET HIM SOMETHIN' TA DRINK! NOW! *(MARGUERITE and BETTY start scrambling inside, hauling JESSIE after them.)*

BETTY. Come on come on come on come on...*(The WOMEN are gone. TOM recovers.)*

BIG ALBERT. What in hell's got into you, boy?

TOM. You stopped me just in time! You hadn't, I'da gone off! I'm a livin' bomb!

BIG ALBERT. Oh, Jesus!

TOM. I can't help it! My whole body turns into it! I get powers! Special powers!...Don't know if they come from God or Space. When I go back to bein' myself, I got nothin... I'm nothin'...Almost killed my wife there. You see that?

BIG ALBERT. I saw.

TOM. Powers. Special powers.

BIG ALBERT. Been recognized.

TOM. What?

BIG ALBERT. Your special powers. Special people recognize 'em.

TOM. 'M I gonna get somethin'?

BIG ALBERT. Maybe.

TOM. I am?

BIG ALBERT. Maybe.

TOM. What?

BIG ALBERT. Whatta you want? *(Pause.)*

TOM. Want a dinner. In my honor. Real restaurant. That place down to the Holiday Inn is good. Eat. Wanna eat. Eat everythin' in sight. Get full for once. Never gotten full in a restaurant.

BIG ALBERT. Well, now, I don't know about no dinner.

TOM. How come?

BIG ALBERT. Promotion, maybe.

TOM. Promotion!

BIG ALBERT. Maybe give you your own Club.

TOM. I won't take it! Oh no! Oh no!

BIG ALBERT. Whatsa matter?

TOM. Don't want no promotion!

BIG ALBERT. That's all you get!

TOM. IT'S NOT WHAT I WANT!

BIG ALBERT. You cut it out, boy, or I'll mess you up!

TOM. I can't tell people what to do!

BIG ALBERT. That's the whole idea!

TOM. Who's gonna tell me what to tell them?

BIG ALBERT. You got your own Club, you could do anythin'.

TOM. I got to know what to do in the first place. I don't know that I'll lead 'em in circles! I'll sic 'em on the wrong people! I'll go wild! Oh no, oh no. I don't make decisions! I don't go swimmin' in the mud at night!

BIG ALBERT. Can't turn it down now.

TOM. I am!

BIG ALBERT. You turn it down they gonna think you not a true one a them.

TOM. I am! I am! I am a true one a them!

BIG ALBERT. You gonna turn it down?

TOM. No...

BIG ALBERT. All right, then.

TOM. A plan! A plan just come to me!

BIG ALBERT. Thatta boy.

TOM. We tell all the people we hate they's somethin' in the cities they can't get anywheres else. They all crowd in. We seize the farmland. Seize the water supply. Take it all for ourselves. Terrorize the outskirts so's they's afraid to leave. They go wild. Start robbin' and lootin'. Givin' each other venereal diseases. Tryin' to escape. We pick 'em off one by one as they emerge. Resta them start eatin' each other. Too busy survivin' to notice us quietly movin' into the White House.

(MARGUERITE and BETTY enter. MARGUERITE carries a glass of water and a plate of cookies.)

BETTY. WE'RE BACK!

MARGUERITE *(advances cautiously to TOM with her offerings)*. I f-f-found you some c-cookies too...

TOM. You think I have to eat those?

MARGUERITE. I-I don't know...

TOM (*knocks the plate out of her hand*). I DON'T HAFTA DO NOTHIN' I DON'T WANT! YOU CAN'T GIVE ME NOTHIN' I DON'T WANT! (*MARGUERITE runs to BETTY.*) WE GOT A WAR GOIN' ON HERE, A WAR! WE'RE RISKIN' OUR LIVES AND YOU'RE HAVIN A TEA PARTY! WE ARE IMPORTANT HERE!

BIG ALBERT. He's right there.

TOM. All this time we been alone!

BIG ALBERT. 'Cause nobody would call it what it was!

TOM. Undeclared! Undeclared war!

BIG ALBERT. But now our time is here!

TOM. We on the wave of our time right now!

BIG ALBERT. And you're tryin' to stop us. (*BIG ALBERT advances on the WOMEN; TOM follows.*)

TOM. You're tryin' to stop us.

BIG ALBERT. That's what you were tryin' to do.

TOM. Don't go outa control, now, boy! I can't hold you back!

(*JESSIE emerges, pointing a gun at the MEN.*)

JESSIE. STOP RIGHT THERE! (*MARGUERITE and BETTY scream; the MEN freeze.*)

TOM. Where'd she get that?

BIG ALBERT. She don't know howta use it.

JESSIE. I watched my husband! I been watchin' him for years!

BIG ALBERT. What's she think she's doin'? Huh? (*to BETTY.*) You know what she thinks she's doin'?

BETTY. No, mister, I don't know.

JESSIE. You can't shut me up anymore!

MARGUERITE. I wanna go home!

BETTY. Shut up, Marguerite!

JESSIE. You can't get me out, neither!

BIG ALBERT. One a you girls better talk to her!

BETTY. What'll we say?

TOM. Talk to her! Now!

MARGUERITE. What'll I say?

BETTY. We'll say whatever you want!

MARGUERITE. Just tell us what to say!

JESSIE. I'm not listenin'!

BIG ALBERT. They all in this together!

BETTY. I'm not in anythin'! I'm not with them!

MARGUERITE. I'm not with them either!

TOM. I knew it!

JESSIE (*to MEN*). They don't understand you!

BETTY. Understand what?

MARGUERITE. I don't know I don't know I don't know I
    don't know!

BIG ALBERT. You gonna pay for this!

BETTY. What?

TOM. YOU GONNA PAY!

JESSIE. We don't understand you!

BIG ALBERT. You better understand!

TOM. WE GONNA MAKE YOU UNDERSTAND!

JESSIE. NOBODY UNDERSTANDS YOU! (*The MEN flee,
    reeling with rage. Pause.*)

BETTY. Good lord, good lord, what have you done? What
    have you done?

JESSIE. What?

BETTY. You gave us up!

JESSIE. I had to!

BETTY. It's over! It's all over!

JESSIE. I couldn't help it!

BETTY. They's gonna come back! They's gonna get us for
    real! They know we know. They know we know!

JESSIE. I don't know what came over me.

MARGUERITE. I wanna go home!

BETTY. Are you nuts?

JESSIE. Your husband'll kill you.

MARGUERITE. He tries all the time but he ain't never succeeded.

BETTY. It's not just you anymore! They think we all in this together!

JESSIE. No way outa their opinions! *(BETTY pulls her hip flask out and swigs. JESSIE goes into action; opens the rifle box which is used as a back step, revealing a cache of guns. She takes the guns out one by one; some of them have names inscribed on the barrels.)*

BETTY. Where in hell did those come from?

JESSIE. Ed always kept a few extras around.

BETTY *(examining some of them)*. C. Davis...R. Mason... The Rat...

JESSIE. Pullet. *(She loads and hands a gun to MARGUERITE, who holds it, astounded.)* He kept everybody else's too. *(She pulls more guns and ammo out of the box, maybe some old grenades, flares and wires.)*

MARGUERITE. How come...they never claimed them?

BETTY. Then they'd really be who they are!...Albert in there?

JESSIE. He's in here. *(She finds BIG ALBERT's gun in the box.)*

BETTY. Could I have Roger Mason too? I used to go with him in high school. *(JESSIE hands BETTY two guns; MARGUERITE stares at the gun she's holding.)* I don't know howta work 'em! I don't know howta work 'em!

JESSIE. Just pull the trigger!

MARGUERITE. What?

JESSIE. Marguerite knows about guns.

MARGUERITE. You askin' me to shoot my husband? *(MAR-GUERITE halts; sets her gun down and tries to hightail it out of there.)* Not me! Oh no, oh no, oh no—

BETTY *(raises MARGUERITE's loaded gun and aims it at her).* Freeze, sister!

JESSIE. BETTY!

MARGUERITE. First rule of guns is: never point at anythin' you don't intend to shoot.

BETTY. Got that.

MARGUERITE. You can't keep me here against myself!

BETTY. Try me!

MARGUERITE. You think I'm stayin' here with you two losers, you got another think comin'!

BETTY. So do you, sister! So do you!

MARGUERITE. I'm nothin' without my man! Nothin'! You hear? I don't like myself that much! I don't wanta think about myself! And I don't wanta go workin' for some stranger I hate, doin' somethin' I can't stand! I wanta stay home! I wanta stare at my wallpaper with the roosters on it! I wanta bake and clean and sing and talk to God all day! Go places at night! Places I can't go without a man! He's my ticket! Without him, I'm trapped! I might as well be dead like Jessie! I don't wanta be like you. I'm not givin' all that up! I got a good deal goin' over there! I'm not the fool everybody thinks I am! I'm not the way I act!

BETTY. They's fifty other women lined up to take your man!

JESSIE. He don't needta put up with you!

BETTY. He won't take you back, honey.

JESSIE. Not now.

BETTY. Not after what you didn't do.

MARGUERITE. He don't want nobody but me!

BETTY. One move, sister, one move!

JESSIE. Please don't quarrel, please don't quarrel, I can't stand it when anybody quarrels!

MARGUERITE. I want my husband! Lemme go! I want my man!

BETTY. He'll kill you!

MARGUERITE. That don't mean I still don't want him!

JESSIE. Put the gun down, Betty. We can't keep her here against herself.

BETTY. Doin' it for her own good.

JESSIE. Can't tell a person that. *(MARGUERITE tries to go as BETTY lowers gun.)* Wait! Marguerite, wait! Take your gun! *(She grabs gun from BETTY.)*

MARGUERITE *(terrified)*. Oh, Jessie!

BETTY. Walk fast. Don't look nobody in the eye.

MARGUERITE. Then how'm I gonna tell if somebody's after me?

BETTY. Just men and couples out this late. Couples won't hurt you. Man won't generally go off on you when he's with another woman. But you see a pack a men, you run. You see a man alone, you run again. They not all bad. You got to remember that. But you can't tell the bad from the good. Even in the light. They all look alike. And you can't trust yourself to judge. You'd have to marry 'em all to find out who they really are!

(MARGUERITE exits cautiously with gun pointed ahead of her. JESSIE starts in right away building a fort; she drags junk into a circle. BETTY tries to load guns, swigs from her flask. Suddenly, MARGUERITE returns; BETTY and JESSIE jump, grab up guns and aim them at her, then relax.)

MARGUERITE. My house! My house is locked!

BETTY. Ain't you got a key to your own house?

MARGUERITE. We never lock our house!...I don't have anywhere to go! I don't have anywhere to go!

BETTY. Well, now you gonna hafta stay with us!

JESSIE. You can help me make the beds up. *(JESSIE dumps the sheets out on the ground; MARGUERITE and BETTY look at each other.)*

MARGUERITE. Out here?

JESSIE. Over here'd be good.

BETTY. Jessie, wouldn't it be better if we went in the house?

MARGUERITE. It's freezin' out here!

JESSIE. I don't sleep in the house anymore.

MARGUERITE. I am not sleepin' in the dirt!

JESSIE. Comes out.

BETTY. What's wrong with your house, Jessie?

JESSIE. A house can get blown up.

MARGUERITE. Ohhh, I don't wanna stay here! I don't! I don't! I don't! I don't!

BETTY. I guess we'll be all right!

MARGUERITE. I won't.

BETTY. Yes, you will.

MARGUERITE. They's spiders in the grass!

BETTY. They don't want you! *(MARGUERITE grabs a pile of sheets and goes to a far corner within the fort and sets up her bed; loads guns.)* I guess I'll go over here. *(BETTY sets up her bed as far away from MARGUERITE as she can get; JESSIE goes inside for pillows and returns.)*

MARGUERITE. I feel so sorry for Tom...nothin' he ever does seems to come out right...and now...*I've* left him... that's what I've done...I've left him...what's he gonna do without me? I feel so sorry for him...

BETTY. Don't be stupid!

MARGUERITE. I'm not stupid!

BETTY. Well, for heaven's sake, don't broadcast it!

MARGUERITE. I am sick to death of everybody thinkin' I'm stupid!

JESSIE. They got to, otherwise they won't talk to you.

MARGUERITE. I never wanted to know what I know in the first place.

BETTY. Long as you keep it a secret.

MARGUERITE. Someday I'm gonna explode and die from all I held in.

BETTY. That's how you get back at them. *(Pause.)* Jessie...

JESSIE. What is it?

BETTY. I'm sorry, Jessie, but I can't sleep without the TV.

MARGUERITE. What?

BETTY. I'm sorry, Marguerite, but I haven't slept without the TV since I got one.

JESSIE. I don't know if the cord'll stretch.

MARGUERITE. I never heard of such a thing!

BETTY. Would you try, Jessie? *(JESSIE goes into the house.)*

MARGUERITE. It's only for one night, Betty.

BETTY. I get lonesome at night. This the only thing that cures it.

(JESSIE reenters with old-fashioned TV; sets it up on barricade; turns it on and sets it to face BETTY.)

BETTY. No sound! No sound! *(JESSIE goes back and turns off sound.)* It's the blue light I need. Just the light.

MARGUERITE. I can't sleep with the light on!

BETTY. You'll get used to it real fast. Then you won't be able to live without it. *(BETTY picks up her bed and moves it closer to the TV; MARGUERITE gets up right after her and goes for more guns, then back to her bed, where she settles in, snuggling them; JESSIE does the same. MAR-*

GUERITE moves her bed in between BETTY and JESSIE; BETTY moves her bed in between MARGUERITE and JESSIE; MARGUERITE and BETTY have a brief pillow fight, then settle down, snuggling in with all the guns. JESSIE sits up to take the first watch. The shadow of light appears in its most distinct form yet; JESSIE stares straight at it; it doesn't waver.)

JESSIE. I gave up Hollywood...I'm one of the few who ever got out. They's hundreds and thousands of others just like me still back there. I hadta leave 'em all behind. I got so sick...so sick of all those jackasses tellin' me howta act... *(She brings the gun up, readies it; keeps watch. Blackout.)*

SCENE TWO

AT RISE: *Next day, early afternoon. JESSIE sits up, embracing the TV; MARGUERITE and BETTY still lie sleeping. MARGUERITE begins to moan and flail from a bad dream; BETTY wakes, tries to waken her.*

BETTY. Marguerite!...Marguerite! Wake up! Wake up, dammit!

MARGUERITE *(comes to, jumping, terrified)*. What? What?...Are we dead?

BETTY. I don't think so.

MARGUERITE. How come?

BETTY. I don't know. I fell asleep!

MARGUERITE. I had a bad dream!

BETTY. 'Course *you* did.

MARGUERITE. I dreamt my whole body went after me. My hand went for my throat, my legs was kickin' my face in...

all my limbs jerked in separate directions and broke my back and my brain spilled outa my mouth like a doily!

BETTY. You all right now.

MARGUERITE. I am not! I'm not all right!

BETTY. Well, get yourself a drinka water.

MARGUERITE. Jessie, could I have a drinka water? *(No answer.)*

BETTY. Jessie? *(No answer; BETTY and MARGUERITE look at each other.)*

MARGUERITE. Jessie! I just gotta have a drinka water! I had a bad dream!

BETTY. Jessie, don't watch so close.

MARGUERITE. You'll get the pinkeye. That's what they say.

BETTY. Woo-woo!

MARGUERITE. What's on?

BETTY. Must be good.

JESSIE. Somebody shot the president. *(Pause.)*

MARGUERITE. What?

BETTY. What?

MARGUERITE. That's not right.

BETTY. You go back and watch again.

JESSIE. Somebody shot the president! *(MARGUERITE and BETTY look at each other a moment, then cram in before the TV.)*

BETTY. What's happenin'? What's happenin'?

JESSIE. I can't see!

MARGUERITE. You're too close to the picture to see!

JESSIE. I see cars stopped on the highways. I see waitresses comin' to a halt with plates in their hands. They's people runnin'...crawlin' over one another...there's the government...they not at their desk...they's watchin' TV! Is America closed?

MARGUERITE. Let me see! Let me see!

BETTY. Wouldn't they a told us?

MARGUERITE. Not with the communists listenin' to our every word! *(Pause; they watch.)*

JESSIE. Oh my lord oh my lord oh my lord oh my lord—

MARGUERITE. What?

BETTY. He's dead.

JESSIE. He's dead he's dead he's dead—

BETTY. Oh my lord oh my lord oh my lord oh my lord...

JESSIE *(joining in)*. Oh my lord oh my lord oh my lord oh my lord...*(BETTY and JESSIE continue their keening; MARGUERITE feels nothing but confusion. The keening comes to an impasse.)* Who's gonna take care of us?

MARGUERITE. Johnson's there!

JESSIE. I don't want Johnson!

BETTY. That's all right, honey, you don't hafta have him!

MARGUERITE. Nobody else wants him, either!

JESSIE. What're we gonna do? What're we gonna do?... We're all alone! We're all alone! *(Pause.)*

MARGUERITE. His wife!

BETTY. Oh, his wife!

MARGUERITE. What's she gonna do without him?

BETTY. She's gonna hafta move!

MARGUERITE. That beautiful house!

BETTY. Where's she gonna go?

MARGUERITE. She got parents! She can move in with them!

JESSIE. She'll learn what to do. I did. *(Pause.)*

MARGUERITE *(gently)*. Jessie, honey, your husband isn't dead.

JESSIE. It's just like it.

MARGUERITE. Don't worry, baby, he'll come back.

JESSIE. He ain't never comin' back!

MARGUERITE. Tom says they's gonna get him off!

JESSIE. No, they ain't!

MARGUERITE. Yes, they will!

JESSIE. No, they ain't!

MARGUERITE. They can't prove what he did.

JESSIE. They got witnesses!

BETTY. No, they don't!

MARGUERITE. You don't know that for sure.

JESSIE. I know!

BETTY. No, you don't.

MARGUERITE. Not for sure!

JESSIE. He's my husband!

MARGUERITE. He was always at my house!

JESSIE. That don't mean you know him!

MARGUERITE. I saw him more than you did!

JESSIE. I'm the one turned him in! *(Long, astonished pause.)*

MARGUERITE. What?

BETTY. Shut up!

MARGUERITE. What did she say?

JESSIE. I'm tired of shuttin' up!

BETTY. Somebody's gonna hear you!

JESSIE. That's who I am!

MARGUERITE. Not you! Not you!

JESSIE. That's who I am!

BETTY. SOMEBODY'S GONNA HEAR YOU! *(Pause.)*

MARGUERITE. Who's gonna take care of you? How you gonna live? Where you gonna go?

BETTY. She'll be all right.

MARGUERITE. She broke the oath! *(Pause. MARGUERITE and BETTY face each other.)*

BETTY. She didn't swear to it!

MARGUERITE. You're not standin' up for her! She lured your husband over here!

JESSIE. I didn't invite 'em!

MARGUERITE. She asked for what they did to her!

JESSIE. Why would I do that?

MARGUERITE. So's you could take down every word!

BETTY. But nobody understood what anybody said!

MARGUERITE. You tell the government anythin' about my husband, anythin', I'll deny you! I'll set the men on you! I'll tell them what you done!

JESSIE. The government'll protect me!

BETTY. Ain't no government! Government's dead!

JESSIE. They still put away murderers!

MARGUERITE. I DON'T WANT TO BE ALONE! (*Sound of glass breaking inside house.*)

BETTY (*panicked*). What was that? (*She drops her gun in fear.*)

JESSIE. Somebody's in the house!

BETTY. What do we do? What do we do?

MARGUERITE. Pick up your gun! Pick up your gun!

JESSIE. It a bomb? Somebody bombin' my house?

MARGUERITE. Over here! Over here! Hurry! Betty! You cover the side! Jessie! You cover the back! (*MARGUERITE herds them together in a circle; they position themselves back to back, their guns pointing out in all directions; JESSIE points hers at the audience.*)

BETTY. Nobody ever taught me howta shoot this thing!

MARGUERITE (*undoes the safety on BETTY's gun for her*). You hafta wait for somebody to come along and teach you, you never gonna learn nothin' in this world!

BETTY. I never wanted to 'til now!

BIG ALBERT (*from house*). Jessie?

TOM (*from alley*). Jessie?

BETTY. It's them, it's them!

MARGUERITE. Point your gun! Point your gun! Jessie! Point your gun!

JESSIE. Who they gonna be this time?

(The MEN enter in street clothes.)

BIG ALBERT. Afternoon, ladies.

TOM. M-M-M-M-Marguerite. *(Pause. MARGUERITE considers her options; looks back at BETTY and JESSIE as she sets her gun down and runs to TOM.)*

MARGUERITE *(as if saved)*. TOM! *(MARGUERITE and TOM embrace and kiss deeply; BIG ALBERT approaches BETTY ominously.)*

BETTY. How'd you get in the house?

BIG ALBERT. Door broke...You pointin' that gun at me?

BETTY. We thought you were somebody else. *(BIG ALBERT takes her gun.)* You mad?

BIG ALBERT. I worried when you didn't come home last night.

(ED comes out of the house.)

BETTY. Oh my Lord Jesus!

BIG ALBERT. Got a present for you, Jessie.

TOM. She's af-f-fraid a wh-what w-w-w-e g-got.

BIG ALBERT. All right, now, Jessie, put down that gun. That's a good girl.

ED. That my wife over there in that red dress? *(JESSIE whirls around, pointing her gun at ED.)*

BIG ALBERT. Now just take it easy, honey.

TOM. Sh-she d-don't recognize him!

BIG ALBERT. She just don't believe it. *(To BETTY.)* Time you came home and made me somethin' ta eat, huh?

BETTY *(terrified)*. Oh, Albert, can't we stay just a little bit longer?

BIG ALBERT. Nope. *(He pulls BETTY off; she looks back at JESSIE.)*

MARGUERITE. I guess we'll be goin' too...Tom...Tom... don't stare...*(She cajoles TOM into leaving.)*

TOM. Ed...J-J-Jessie...*(MARGUERITE and TOM exit; ED and JESSIE face off.)*

ED. That right? You don't believe it?

JESSIE. How...how did you get out?

ED. Somebody made a mistake...But it's all right now... Everythin's under control. *(Slowly he comes forward and takes the gun.)* Saw Lenny Hemmel in the jail a couple weeks ago...And Bobbie Jones...used to live next door? He was in there too. And Tom's cousin Cash. Saw him practically every day. They all say hello.

JESSIE. That's nice.

ED. Yeah...*(He wanders around the yard.)* Ya miss me? *(He looks at her; she looks down, shrugs, admits it; nods vigorously.)* What'd you do around here while I was gone?

JESSIE. Nothin'.

ED. Looks different.

JESSIE. 'S the same.

ED. Somethin's changed.

JESSIE. I know who you are. *(Pause.)*

ED. Don't matter...don't matter to nobody...so...here we go again...

JESSIE. Uh-huh.

ED. Well...I'll see ya...

JESSIE *(with renewed strength)*. Where ya goin'? Ed? *(ED halts; looks at her.)* Where you goin'? *(Blackout.)*

END OF PLAY

DIRECTOR'S NOTES

DIRECTOR'S NOTES

DIRECTOR'S NOTES

DIRECTOR'S NOTES

DIRECTOR'S NOTES

DIRECTOR'S NOTES